Wilted Sorrows

Sienna C. Jones

Copyright © 2025 by Sienna C. Jones

Photography by Sofia Alonso

All rights reserved.

No part of this book may be reproduced in any form or by any electronic or mechanical means, including information storage and retrieval systems, without written permission from the author, except for the use of brief quotations in a book review.

Book layout by Rein G.

To those with sensitive hearts.

A collection of words drowning
in the fragility of time.

CONTENTS

i.

youth
the burden of you
early days
a worrier
writer
worthy
a journal entry #1
my birth was the crime
healing
uneasiness
out of the blue

ii.

anxious, i am
a heart bleeds
my faith
i surrender
time
our honest cries
to write a letter
my final cry
the work you created
emotion
when you find my letter
self portrait

iii.

a journal entry #2
curse of an age
tomorrow
the river
i remember
nostalgia
doves
mother
what died never wills to stay dead
on display
to wash your bones
air of the past

i. Caged Youth

'Every page that I wrote, you were on it,'

— Gracie Abrams, *Free Now*

Sienna C. Jones

Memories cascade through open stares,
childhood engraves itself into our fingerprints.
Tick, tick, the coward roars—
but oh, the mirror mourns.

Age is but a fortune when the lines are true,
yet the youth, withers, and so do you.
Once a lion, pride paints your pounce,
now an act, with a crack, I note your crouch.

Stems are longer; the pit creeps deeper;
my knees, scarring a plead to the timekeeper.
I gave it my all — I vow to him.
I gave it my all — I murmur in the hymn.

Bear to her chest, the dagger deepens,
beneath the skin, an ode to my existence.
Memories cascade through open stars,
my **youth** is but a scar haunting my spine.

My blood's wrath stems further
than his fingertips. It threads
the bones of his youth,
and with age it unravels.

No touch can sort these knots,
for they come to etch
the questions into the headstones.

The mirrors taunt me with eyes
unlike mine:
with wrinkles that ripple
with the grief of before.

One sun. One moon. Pity
lining their breaths, for I am
watched as I watch the eyes of another.

These scars are old,
these wounds are new.
I cannot, and will not,
forget **the burden of you**.

Wilted Sorrows

Heavy irises dancing in the breeze,
with songs of sorrow swallowing the ease.
Counting on stars, one, two, three,
I long for the **early days** of me.

Naivety scattering over my bones,
perhaps I laid in the womb of a clone.
Had she held the heart of a soldier,
would I still long for the days when I'm older?

My knees are scratched, and scarred, and skinned,
but oh, there goes, my phantom of sins.
She is beauty, she is breath,
she would've once dared to have actually left.

Wilted Sorrows

A worrier, the words, like lace,
are woven through the braid
of my guarded spine.

The wind picks up, the hair
unravels. The phantoms
fall into their waltz.

They taunt, they cheer, I cry –
still, none hear such a sound.
None hear the sirens of my name.

I swear, they're pointing – Oh, look!
They're pointing! Like a circus,
and a clown. They're pointing.

Sienna C. Jones

By the graves of the poets
my melodies sing;
they hear my lullabies.

Writer

Wilted Sorrows

Child, oh, child,
carry me whole.
Gift me my grave,
lay out my coal.

Has my life been **worthy** –
full of blessed return?
Or, have I not been sturdy
with my head-high burn?

I dare to argue differently,
set my view ablaze.
I've fought sufficiently,
dare to doubt my claim?

A journal entry #1:

A river guides the young when the world lacks the eye for sensitivity. Except, upstream is where the heart of all creation lies, for she knows the battle of emotion. None should fear the crease of their eyes, the dimples of their cheeks, the lines of age that only so few are fortunate enough to see. So long, I journeyed downstream, passing the trees that nod. So long, I overlooked the beat that made me human. I did not care to look over my shoulder. I did not care to note that I was good. I did not care to be good if I felt as I was feeling. I was feeling, far too much. So, I trekked downstream; and stumbled over rocks as the currents memorised my spine. Following the flow of the water, life passed me by.

By, a fish opposed me. A fish, of all creatures! It swam by my leg, towards the heart I did not want to know. I turned my head to scowl, but then I spotted it. The child, that was me. She stood far, estranged, disappointed in the water flowing through my fingers. She ran, I yelled, I fell. Submerged, the daughter of I sinks opposite me, and I reach for her. I pull her into the air, and hand in hand, we start the trek towards the heart. It's hard, and all point the other way. But, so long have I neglected this heart, this girl, so long that I don't recognise the reflection of my gaze. I don't recognise the heartless.

It begins with you holding my hand,
except, excuse me, but I can never understand –
why you must pick up that fatal blade,
and claim my life, as if we only have today.

We once waltzed and sang as if all was well,
now, I clasp and claw at my shell.
Engraving sorrow into my skin, my bones,
I watch you change your many thrones.

Why was today burdened, and tomorrow promised?
All I wanted was for you not to be dishonest.
I plead, I cry, I wait, I smile,
yet, I cannot stand this wretched trial.

The people asked what changed this time,
Except —how am I to say that **my birth was the crime**?
I wait as time takes its toll,
and one by one, I lose my soul.

They assume I shall be used to this,
so why am I trapped in this endless abyss?
It's a game! One says. A play! They chant.
I wonder when I will be freed from this trance.

Sienna C. Jones

I once queried if your heart
will still beat for me in the winter.
If your lungs will still breathe
for me in the noon.

Now, my chest is lighter,
and the stars, brighter.
Victim of time no longer,
and a victim of mine ignored.

You pass me in the streets, a simple
glance; turning away with a nod.
Recognition heavy on your lips,
your lungs faithful to God.

I knew the memories were blinding,
consistent on your journey home.
With lightness I hope you share
the **healing** I condone.

An **uneasiness** hangs in the air
between my chest and my knees.
A friend, or foe, I would not
trust the maze of my fingertips
without her.

Sienna C. Jones

Out of the blue,
a story old as time.
Out of the blue,
a story that's mine.

Out of the blue,
you came.
Out of the blue,
no game.

Out of the blue,
we met.
Out of the blue,
no longer I fret.

ii. Mirrored Palms

'I need a father, I need a mother, I need some older, wiser being to cry to. I talk to God, but the sky is empty, and Orion walks by and doesn't speak.'

— Sylvia Plath, *The Unbridged Journals of Sylvia Plath*

Sienna C. Jones

A tender heart, I hold my love,
a blessing woven through the emotions
of the anxious – **anxious, I am**.

Fear takes the body of a phantom,
a breath in the wake of night.
In my nightgown, I chase such a soul,
but a maze is my mind.

Right now, I am myself.
I feel,
like myself.
To be free, is to not to be me.

My heart, my armour, I defy
such phantoms as their tongues boil.
I love. I love. I love.
I will not fight.

A tender heart, my emotion sits,
holding a thread, a needle, and Time.
My phantoms sit by, watching – waiting.

When will she stitch her wounds shut? They ask.

Woven through the threads of my sleeve,
a heart bleeds, then beats, then bleeds.
The armour she bears grows tired,
with the sleeve beginning to unravel.

The heart waltzes on the threads of time,
fingers weaving through all passing by;
surrendering to the nights when they arise,
she plucks the harp of such a lullaby.

Her bones cage the fragility of the age.
Her skin clings to the stability of the stage.
White knuckled hands hold the sword of emotion,
and I dance with deep devotion.

The arrows they come coaxed in my blood,
familiar eyes behind everyone.
Questions and confusion shape a battle cry,
and I try – all I do is try.

The seamstress sits waiting, front row,
tugging on the threads of my heart –
she, the artist, behind the bow.
The arrows, words I could never write…
Still, they're signed by the spotlight.

Wilted Sorrows

Carving the branches into crosses,
I search for **my faith** in the splinters
of my palms.

Winter comes, the nights are young,
my breath smothers the days – I write
to Him.

Answers, fail. Rain becomes
heavy. Thick, the stench of my childhood
window sill.

Bruises long gone, I bury the
prayers in the dirt of my nails.

Sienna C. Jones

I've connected the cracks of my fingertips,
I've listened to the hymn of my heartbeat,
I've engraved my name into the boulder of my stomach;
still, Time allows the ripping of my hair.

Nails are short, splintered, broken, bitten,
I remain the common enemy.
Skin: bruised, swollen, scratched,
a forbidden maze with the history of my longing.

Journals are torn, pages are written;
an exhale of yesterday, and the day before,
these words are familiar, a silhouette of a friend.
A friend, a friend, a friend?

Night is old, my fan rattled, the cars pass,
I seek the path of the veins in my arms.
I blame them for the brushstrokes of my fingers,
the ballad of my heartbeat, the waltz of my stomach.

I blame –

The stars put on a film that only exhaust carries.

My youth is cradled, my head is kissed.

I am a daughter/a child/a soul.

I am someone, not one, but another.

Light creeps beneath the bedroom door,

I toss, I turn.

Your voice is far as it is near,

I call to it, **I surrender**.

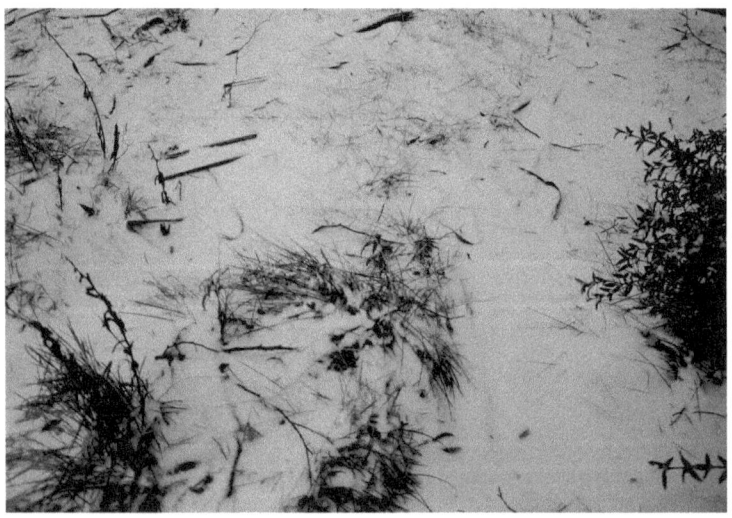

Perched on my window sill, Time
bore no expression to his lips.
Like mine, his hands were calloused,
stained with the ink from the past.

Letter after letter, it was rehearsed –
a performance. I write to the sea of me.
Every ripple is every Age, and with Age
comes a wave. Each wave, a reminder:
Time yearns to heal. Heal?

Time's knees bleed, but no longer
is forgiveness sought. Medallions hang
from the throats of the unworthy,
gold beneath their nails.

Crescents bine the words I write;
Time collects the pages, holding the thread
unravelling truth. The sky darkens,
storms come, I seek my identity
in the rippling water.

A face I do not know stares.

Sienna C. Jones

The moon humbles **our honest cries**,
noting the fractured rhythm of our breaths.
Strip me of my security, I say.
Watch my bones emerge, and perhaps
then a lie won't haunt my tongue.

The moon humbles our honest cries,
noting the ivy written glances.
Strip me of my emotions, I say.
Watch my chest heave, and perhaps
then the truthful blood will spill.

Sienna C. Jones

To write a letter, immortalising every deed to have engraved my flesh. To write a letter, carving my experience into my name. To write a letter, then will the desperation neglect the mockery? My skin, can be skin, without the sins, and yet I brand myself with such a title, and the stars pity the search for an acknowledgment. To write a letter, will my words go heard? **To write a letter**, will the words find the page?

Wilted Sorrows

Shall I be enough for you,
if they bruise my bones in two?
Rip me of my anguished despair
and I'll be yours if only you cared.

The sea quivers, the tides turn,
my ships sink, inevitably, I burn.
They sing, they shout, they scream, they praise!
Just as you always seem to betray.

My heart mourns; I cling to the sheets.
When, oh, when, will I finally weep?
Time turns, dawn arises,
when will I claim these apparent prizes?

You claim it's love, I bellow a lie,
tell me, when will you hear **my final cry**?
Time to reverse, and capture me whole.
Yet, I fear, I have now lost all control.

Bones cracking and shifting, a golden crimson seeping through. No longer do I stand as **the work you created**, as the stone that holds the memories of all the hours that were ours: all the seconds where your touch was mine, and you worked to bring to life the beauty we both knew lingered within my soul. No longer am I beauty nor art. For now, you stare at me as if I am deception. You cling to every shard, every splinter – remnants of us haunting your every breath. Whether that be the clay beneath your nails or the brushes doomed forevermore with the brushstrokes marking my wounded bones. You knew me, you created me, and then you shattered me. I was high, the plinth my stage, and then one slip and pieces of my youth scattered across every corner of this palace. You heard me beg to be as I was – to be as innocent as I was. Yet, you stood there before fleeing – aware that all was lost, I was lost. Now, the moon watched through the windows as I'm left to take a new form. A new life. One with no familiarity. To change is the truest art of them all. One that only you can control.

Sienna C. Jones

Irises painted with familiarity,
you note the crumble to my stone.
Still, you chisel, carving me into
the sensitivity only art can understand.

Emotion, my pedestal...
Avert your eyes!
Avert them, I say!

The ash of my existence cascades
past yours. Still, am I weak to stumble,
the mess you made. Fragile,
I cannot stand — you hold the blade.

Wilted Sorrows

When you find my letter, please tell me:

has my handwriting changed?

Or did the words paint a portrait

of a past you neglect to reflect?

When you find my letter, please tell me:

did a familiar voice toy with

the hairs on your arms? Or did

a song of such pride blind your mind?

When you find my letter, know that I am

free now. The words are the last that I

will write:

I no longer desire a fight.

A little tragedy born a weapon...
One who bears crimson flowers.

Self Portrait

iii. Gave You All

'I dwell in Possibility,'

— Emily Dickinson, *I Dwell in Possibility*

A journal entry #2:

Only in the lines of my palms do yesterday and tomorrow meet. In Time, they change – but don't we all? Only in the lines of my palms do I sit, cross legged and talk to myself. Both the girl and woman, they sit opposite me, braiding their hair with the ribbons of Time. We marvel at the gaps in our teeth, the crease of our cheeks, and the constellations of our experiences. We marvel as Time stands near, in awe at our survival. I step into the gallery of our irises and take in all that we have done, and that we have lived. I hold onto the hands of yesterday and tomorrow, and I vow to do them proud. I will do them proud.

Woven, but a **curse of an age**. A tether holds us
bound for a phantom is crucified to your
name. Rust lingers in your words, a vow to your
touch. Lust shivers in the stolen stars, a forbidden
law in the decade of you. Plaguing my mind, the
stars study such a child.

I sit.

    I sit.

        I sit.

I wait.

The ivy memorises my shape, and your entrance is
grand. Words of man mimic a battlefield, but my naivety
only surrenders to their hand. Awareness of both
self, and you, can only stitch so much. My wounds
continue to weep, an endless cycle of the thrill. You
slip through the bars into the words I write.

A sin.

    A sin.

A sin, the preachers mourn. They know the tale;
the one in which an age such as mine is echoed.
Longing, yearning, lusting. The wind will change
tomorrow. For now, I turn my chin towards the
unknowing, in the breeze.

Gold layering the hours lost,
Tomorrow's but a turn of page.
She lies with me at nightfall,
and grabs the paint when stars fall.

Such promise is Tomorrow,
such splendour in her hand.
I forget my lined palms,
my exhausted eyes.
I forget the stone carved by
my naivety.

Tomorrow creates the more.
It frames it, shields it;
Tomorrow lines the path I walk with pebbles.

Sienna C. Jones

Thunder smothering the mountaintops,
forests hide the august skies.
Like pictures in a forgotten album,
these memories come to me like
the tides changing in **the river**.

My hair is wet with yesterday,
my skin is damp with tomorrow.
I crouch, knees to my open chest.
The breeze welcomes a stranger,
unaware of the child to her touch.

Years pass, and eventually,
I walk up stream, fighting the currents,
a fallen victim. Your voice
waltzes through the leaves.

Transcending beneath our nails,
the soil whispers of the time before us;
of the people who carved the turn
of my time.

Names demolished, their touch lines
the bones of the brushstrokes studied.
Chip of my tooth. Scar to my finger.
Dimple to my cheek.

I see the art, **I remember**.
I see the creations, I vouch my prayers.
Connected, all souls one,
I teach what I know — craft what I forget.

Nostalgic, for the rays of the winter sun startling the stained glass. Nostalgic, for the creak in the floorboards that haunt the young. Nostalgic, for the glisten once making her bed in the breath of my irises. Nostalgic, a phantom mirroring my hand in the wake of the night. Nostalgic, I follow in every reflection, every scent.

Nostalgia, she holds my hand in death, and carves my name on my casket.

Once a lone dancer, now three

more before me. They line the stage

with roses, they carve praises into

the seats watching such a performance.

Doves, they were; a flaw for each one.

The thorns, they pricked them, they pricked them

again! Flaws, for each one – but,

they pass me the roses, they pass them

to me!

A button nose, a wrinkled lip,
A crease of the eyes, a curved hip.
My knees are bruised, healed tomorrow.
My skin is used, known and borrowed.

History and Time define my every breath,
I write and dedicate this to all who left.
The doves they pass, I watch them fly,
still I'm accused of every white lie.

You came before me, experienced this before,
a spell of a **mother** cursed with folklore.
I'll wield the sword, in all of my strength,
and I will fight beyond such drastic lengths.

Through the whispers in the wind, I hear them
chant. **What died never wills to stay dead –**
your laugh is in the colour of my eyes, your smile
beams within the beat of my heart. Your touch is in the braid
of my hair, and your love flows in the courage of my
steps. The words will be written, and the seasons,
they'll change. Frost will familiar itself with my
surroundings, and one night it will reveal to me a
handprint that cannot be mine.

Time, a mere illusion,
I'm back where I began. What died never wills
to stay dead. You're all around me: in my every breath.
Even with wilting skin your face stains the mirrors
and I smile at an old friend that I will see again.

Sienna C. Jones

My chest, a stage, my soul, **on display**. Each beat of my heart is the rhythm they must dance – they must hear it echo through their head, as it echoes through mine and they must not miss a beat for there is an arrow at their spine!

To wash your bones,

what would it feel like?

To fill a bucket with water so cold and to submerge
the sins smothering your actuality, what would it
feel like? Collecting your burdens – perhaps cleansing all –
the moon howling above would heal. A hold to crave.
A hold, so gentle. Feeling lighter, your bones will wield
together like a puzzle. Familiar, I know. Steps, no longer
drag.
Once cleansed, summer's breath welcomes
you in the mornings.
Once cleansed, winter's caress bids
you farewell in the evenings. The doves, they pass, but
they note the words I can finally write; as these words
were hidden, and it was only when my bones were
submerged did they reveal themselves to me. To wash my
bones, I studied the engravings in marble, and I
looked up, and bowed my head towards the artist.

Air of the past cascades
the exhales of my present –
removing ownership out
of the hands of sin.

Reluctant at first, the will
passes my wake –
and for once, and for all,
I breathe my name.

Sienna C. Jones
is an author from
Melbourne, Australia.

www.ingramcontent.com/pod-product-compliance
Lightning Source LLC
Chambersburg PA
CBHW042343300426
44109CB00049B/2820